Positive and Inspirational Coloring Book

It is time to open up and flourish

Magical new doors open for me right now!

Great things take time...
Be patient

I CHOOSE TO BE HAPPY

I CHOOSE TO BE EXCITED!

SPRINKLE KINDNESS

EVERYWHERE YOU GO

I GIVE MYSELF PERMISSION
TO SHINE

THERE ARE ENDLESS OPPORTUNITIES BEFORE ME

I am stronger than I believe

Embrace your
sensitivity

Create new opportunities

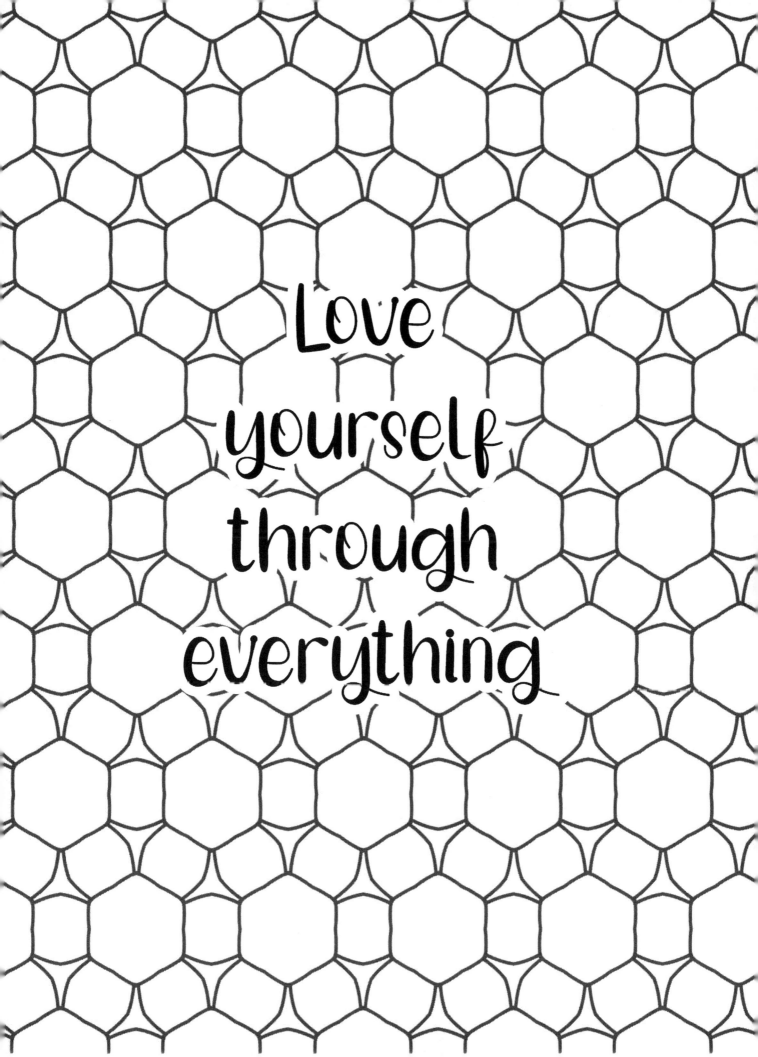

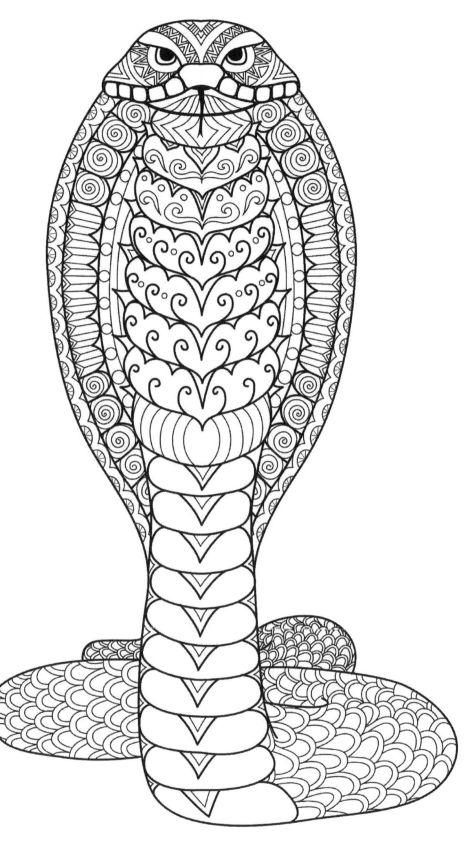

I am bigger than my fears

Laughter is the fireworks of the soul

BE STRONGER THAN YOUR EXCUSES

DO NOT BE PART OF THE PROBLEM.

CHOOSE TO BE PART OF THE SOLUTION

I choose to be grateful

I CAN START OVER AT ANY TIME

Be the reason someone smiles today

Every moment is a fresh beginning

Mistakes are proof that you are trying

Be silly, be honest, be kind

Made in United States
Troutdale, OR
07/05/2024

21033740R00035